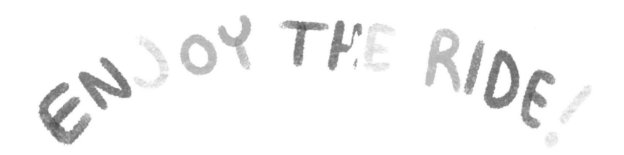

A Book to Help Understand and Cope with Feelings

Dedicated to my family, friends, teachers, and clients

Copyright © 2021 by Kate Stark
ISBN: 978-1-7362913-0-6

About this book:

Life is a journey and emotions guide us through our experiences. Travel along with Fred the feelings chameleon as he helps the reader understand how emotions help us, how they are experienced in our bodies, how our emotions and thoughts are connected, and how to use coping skills when feelings get too big.

At the end of the book are practice worksheets for the reader to draw or write about their feelings and to make an individualized coping skills plan.

Hi there! My name is Fred and I'm a chameleon. Do you want to see my super cool trick? I change colors each time I have a feeling. Yes, I know I am amazing. You are, too! Welcome to a grand adventure. Here is your backpack. Inside there are things you will need. I hope you enjoy the ride!

First stop on our adventure: We are going to a new school. It is your first day and you don't know anyone. Although you are excited, everything is new and different, and you feel kind of jittery. When you find your class, your teacher asks you to stand up in front of everyone, say your name, and tell a fun fact about yourself. When you stand up, you can't think of anything to say and everyone is staring at you.

Hop on the worry coaster! Worry is a word that also means anxious. As you can see, I'm a lovely shade of white when I'm on the worry coaster. What happens to your body when you are worried? Your heart starts to beat fast. Your mouth may get dry. If you are VERY worried, you may even feel kind of dizzy, your tummy may feel funny, and you might even get a headache.

What happens to your thoughts when you are worried? Well, your thoughts might imagine what could go wrong. *"What will other kids think of me? What if they think I'm not cool? What if I mess up my words? What if a dancing banana wearing a top hat bursts through the door?"* Well, just kidding about the banana one. That would be kind of funny.

It's OK to be worried, as long as you know what to do. Worry feelings help keep you safe, like deciding not to go too close to that snarling dog because you are worried it might bite you. Worry feelings also help you anticipate possible problems, like making sure you pack all of your homework because you are worried you will forget it.

BUT....sometimes worry feelings happen when there is not a real danger or problem. Or sometimes your worry feelings last too long, happen too much, or make you feel uncomfortable. So what do you do? Open up your backpack and let me show you some coping skills! Inside you will find tools to manage all of your feelings!

First is an imaginary candle. You can use a real one if you like. I like to use an imaginary one because real candles make me sneeze. AAACHOOO!! Plus, I don't carry candles around. What is this imaginary candle for? Well, it's a coping skill to help your body go from worried to calm by taking slow and deep breaths.

LISTEN CLOSELY! You can't just breathe all willy-nilly and expect things to change. You have to smell your imaginary candle with the BIGGEST and SLOWEST sniff you've ever sniffed. What does your candle smell like? Brownies? Flowers?

Next, you slowly blow out the flame of your imaginary candle. Don't blow like the big, bad, wolf. Blow slowly, like your mouth only opens to the size of a pea. Now, do it again! And again! AND AGAIN! Keep it slow! Do this until you feel your heartbeat slow down and your body feels calm. I take 10 slow, deep breaths when I'm worried, but your number may be 8 or 12. Great job!

Now, it's time to check your thoughts! Did you know that your thoughts are not always true, especially when you have BIG feelings? Yes, when you have a big feeling you may think the worst. Your thoughts mean well, but sometimes you have to lasso your thoughts, rein them in, and give them a good, stern, talk.

When you have big feelings, you need to ask yourself, *"Are my thoughts true? Are my thoughts helpful?"* Here's one of your thoughts. *"What will they think of me?"* Well, it can be good to care what people think of you. That helps you be a good friend and a nice person.

Worrying about if others think something bad or if you will mess up will not help you, and it may not even be true. The kids in your class will probably all be thinking different thoughts, and that's OK. One kid may be excited to hear what you have to say. Another kid may be thinking about how much time is left until lunch. Even if you do mess up your words, what person has never made a mistake?

Either way, a more helpful thought is *"I can do this. I'm going to be myself. This will be over soon, and it will be OK. I can say that I have a cat named Floofers or name my favorite TV show as my fun fact."* What's a fun fact you might say about yourself? Great work!

Next stop on our adventure: You are at your house getting ready for your friend's birthday party. You have been looking forward to it all week. Hooray! I wonder what kind of cake your friend will have. I hope it is chocolate! I bet your friend is going to love the present you bought. Anyway, suddenly your mom comes in and tells you the party is canceled because your friend is sick.

Climb on in the mopey boat! Mopey is a word that means sad. As you can see, I'm a beautiful shade of blue when I'm on the mopey boat. What happens to your body when you get sad? Well, you may feel like you have a lump in your throat. Your eyes may fill up with tears and you might even cry (even better for filling up the river for your mopey boat)! You may feel tired and your body might move slower.

What happens to your thoughts when you are really sad? Well, sad thoughts may make you feel even worse. You may think, *"This is the worst thing that could have happened. The whole day is ruined!"*

It's OK to be on the mopey boat. Sad feelings help you know what you care about. It's OK to let yourself feel sad. But sometimes, your sad feelings may be too big or last for too long. So…you guessed it! Open your backpack and get out your coping skills!

When you are sad, after you let yourself row a little bit on the mopey boat, it may be time to do a coping skill. Inside your backpack you will find a cup of **TEA**. **TEA** stands for 3 good things to do when you are sad.

Talk
Talk to a family member, friend, or someone else you trust.

Enjoy
Do something you **Enjoy** (games, reading, watching funny videos, listening to music, playing with a pet, drawing). What else do you like to do?

Active
Do something **Active**! Dance to a fun song, take a walk, go to the park, or pretend you are the dancing banana!

Now it's time to check those thoughts! Were your sad thoughts helpful or true? The canceled party is disappointing. You have a right to be sad. But, thinking it was the worst thing ever or that your day is ruined probably is not helpful or true. What could you think instead? *"I was really looking forward to the party, but maybe I can do something else fun today. I can also write my friend a note to feel better."* Nice work!!

At our next stop, you are building with some blocks and you have built a tall tower. It looks amazing! HIGH FIVE! You worked really hard on that tower. Suddenly, your brother comes in and falls into your tower, knocking the whole thing down.

All aboard the anger train! *CHOO CHOO!* As you can see, I'm a fiery shade of red when I'm on the anger train. Anger is a word that also means mad.

What happens to your body when you're mad? Well, your heart may beat fast, your muscles may get tight, and you may feel kind of hot. What happens to your thoughts when you are angry? You may think the worst! *"He did that on purpose! That's not fair! I'm going to make him pay!"*

It's OK to be on the anger train, as long as you know what to do and what NOT to do. Angry feelings help you stand up for yourself (or someone else) when something bothers you or does not seem fair. But your anger may be too big, last too long, or make you feel bad. It's important not to let your anger take over because you might do something that makes it worse, like yelling or hitting.

Time to open up that backpack! Here is a pretend space suit. Do you really need a space suit? No, it's to help you remember to "take space." When you are *very* angry, the best thing to do is take some space, which means going to take a break by yourself and get some space away from whatever made you mad.

Take some space in a quiet area where you can take some slow, deep breaths (use that pretend brownie candle if you want) so your body and mind can calm down. Where can you take space where you live? What if you're at school and you get mad? Well, you may not be able to run out of the classroom to take space. You could ask to get a drink of water or take some deep breaths at your desk.

THEN, go back and say how you feel in a calm voice. "Brother, I worked really hard on those blocks. It really upset me when you knocked them down. Can you help me build my tower again?" But…here's the thing: Your brother may say he is sorry, or he may laugh and say "MUAHAHA I am the block destroyer!!" You can't control your brother. You can only control what YOU do. If you get back at him, you will probably get in trouble, the problem won't be solved, and you may not feel any better. If you stand up for yourself and it doesn't work out, you may need to take some space again, go play a different game, or ask an adult for help.

What about your thoughts? You can say things like: *"I can go calm down first and decide what to do or how to share my feelings. My anger is not the boss of me."* These words can help you be calm and solve your problem. Way to go!

Well, friend, I hope you enjoyed our ride. I hope you learned that it is OK to have different feelings. You will probably take more rides on the worry coaster, mopey boat, or anger train.

If you do, try some coping skills from your backpack if the feeling is too big. You may learn some more coping skills along your journey. Well, it's time for me to go. See you later, alligator!

About the Author:

Kate Stark, PhD is a licensed psychologist and licensed specialist in school psychology in Fort Worth, Texas. She specializes in providing therapy and assessment for children. She has worked in various settings including schools, hospitals, community mental health, nonprofit, and private practice. Dr. Stark's passion for use of humor and metaphors in therapy inspired her to write this book. Dr. Stark lives in Fort Worth with her husband and two children.
Website:
www.katestarkphd.com/

About the Illustrator:

Shawn Melchor is a Concept artist and has been working in the entertainment industry for 10+ years. In 2009 Shawn started his career as a Concept artist at Disney's Junction Point Studios where he worked on the critically acclaimed Epic Mickey and the sequel Epic Mickey 2: The power of two. A diligent and multi-talented artist, Shawn created digital and traditional works for the Character Designs, Environments, as well as a multitude of Visual Development and Marketing art needs.
Facebook art page:
https://m.facebook.com/Melchor.Shawn/
ArtStation art page:
https://pest3r.artstation.com/

What makes you **happy**?

Write about it or draw a picture:

_____

_____

_____

_____

_____

What makes you **worried**?

Write about it or draw a picture:

_____

_____

_____

_____

_____

What makes you **sad**?

Write about it or draw a
picture:

_____

_____

_____

_____

_____

What makes you **angry**?

Write about it or draw a picture:

_____

_____

_____

_____

_____

_____

My Coping Skills Plan:

Worried:	Sad:
How many deep breaths will I take?	Who can I **talk** to about my sad feelings?
Who can I talk to about my worried feelings?	What do I **enjoy** doing that might help me feel better?
What is a helpful thought I can think when I'm worried?	What do I like to do that is **active**?
Angry:	
Where can I take space where I live? What is a helpful thought I can think when I'm angry?	

Made in the USA
Coppell, TX
22 January 2021

48604488R00017